PAPERBACK **PLUS**

Table of Contents

Sheep in a Shop 7
a story by Nancy Shaw
illustrated by Margot Apple

Sheep 33
a poem by Mike Thaler

Happy Birthday! 34
an invitation and a thank-you note

Let's Visit the Shop 36
a photo essay about a museum shop

Meet Nancy Shaw

Once Nancy Shaw was playing a rhyming game with her children. She thought of the words *sheep* and *jeep* and got an idea for a book — *Sheep in a Jeep*. Now there are more books about those sheep.

Meet Margot Apple

Margot Apple loves animals. Here she is riding a horse. She also likes to draw funny animals. One day in art class she even made a clay pot with animal feet!

Sheep in a Shop

Nancy Shaw

Sheep in a Shop

Illustrated by Margot Apple

HOUGHTON MIFFLIN COMPANY
BOSTON
ATLANTA   DALLAS   GENEVA, ILLINOIS   PALO ALTO   PRINCETON

Also by Nancy Shaw and illustrated by Margot Apple:

Sheep in a Jeep
Sheep on a Ship

Acknowledgments

For each of the selections listed below, grateful acknowledgment is made for permission to excerpt and/or reprint original or copyrighted materials, as follows:

Selections

Sheep in a Shop, by Nancy Shaw, illustrated by Margot Apple. Text copyright © 1991 by Nancy Shaw. Illustration copyright © 1991 by Margot Apple. Reprinted by permission of Houghton Mifflin Company. All rights reserved.

"Sheep," by Mike Thaler. Copyright © 1992 by Mike Thaler. Reprinted by permission of the author.

Illustrations

33 Denise Y Fernando. **36** Courtesy of The Children's Museum, Boston (inset).

Photography

ii Larry E. Wright/Ann Arbor News Photo/Courtesy of Nancy Shaw (t); Courtesy of Margot Apple (b). **34** (inset), **35** (inset) Banta Digital Group. **34–35** (background) Tony Scarpetta. **36, 37, 38** Tracey Wheeler.

To Fred, for suggesting a birthday theme, to Scott, for sharing many happy birthdays, and to my parents, for making birthdays possible.

—N.S.

For these sheep-loving shopkeepers: Anne; Barbara & Art; Claire, David & Diana; Cree, Ann & Marcia; Jan; Janet; Leslie & Maude; Linda; Mark; Michael; Nancy.

—M.A.

A birthday's coming! Hip hooray!

Five sheep shop for the big, big day.

9

Sheep find rackets. Sheep find rockets.

Sheep find jackets full of pockets.

Sheep find blocks.

Sheep wind clocks.

Sheep try trains. Sheep fly planes.

14

Sheep decide to buy a beach ball.

Sheep prefer an out-of-reach ball.

Sheep climb. Sheep grumble.

Sheep reach. Sheep fumble.

Sheep sprawl.

Boxes tumble.

Boxes fall in one big jumble.

19

Sheep put back the beach ball stack.

They choose some ribbon

from the rack.

They dump their bank. Pennies clank.

22

There's not enough to buy this stuff.

Sheep blink. Sheep think.

What can they swap to pay the shop?

25

Sheep clip wool, three bags full.

Sheep trade.

The bill is paid.

29

Sheep hop home in the warm spring sun.

They're ready for some birthday fun.

SHEEP

When sheep
Can't sleep
Do they make a big fuss,
Or do they just go ahead
And begin
To count
Us?

by Mike Thaler

33

Happy Birthday!

A Party!

Dear ___Kate___,
Please come to my
___birthday party___.
Day: ___Sunday, May 6___
Time: ___1:00 P.M.___
Place: ___44 Maple Street___

Your friend,

Ann

Thank You!

Dear Kate,
    Thank you for the book
about cats. The pictures
are so funny!
                    Love,
                    Ann

El Mercado del Barrio
Neighborhood Market

Vegetables
Vegetales

Carnes

Let's Visit

the Shop

WHAT'S WHERE
Visitor Guide to The Children's Museum, Boston

THIRD FLOOR

Jana and Tommy are visiting a playtime shop at The Children's Museum. It's a placc where kids can learn to shop for food. What kinds of foods are in the shop? How much does each kind cost?

pineapples
—
ananás
9¢

apples
—
manzanas
4¢

lemons
—
limones
3¢

oranges
—
naranjas
6¢

Jana is dressed up as a shopkeeper. How many things is Tommy pretending to buy? How much money will he have to pay?